Grace Murray Hopper

Working to Create the Future

Sofwest Press
Las Cruces, NM, USA

LIVES WORTH LIVING

Grace Murray Hopper

Working to Create the Future

by

Carl J. Schneider and Dorothy Schneider

NEW ENGLAND
PUBLISHING
ASSOCIATES

Copyright © 1998 by New England Publishing Associates, Inc. and Carl J. Schneider and Dorothy Schneider.

Produced by New England Publishing Associates, Inc. for SOFSOURCE, Inc.

Series Editor: Edward W. Knappman
Copy Editing: Miccinello Associates
Design and Page Composition: Ron Formica
Photo Researcher: Victoria Harlow
Editorial Administration: Ron Formica and Christopher Ceplenski
Proofreading: Doris Troy

Cover Design: Gabriel Quesada
Cover Photo: Organ Mountains at Sunrise, Las Cruces, NM; Frank Parrish

ISBN 1-57163-606-4

Library of Congress Catalog Card Number: 98-84770
Printed in the United States of America
01 00 99 98   9 8 7 6 5 4 3 2

The Lives Worth Living *Series consists of biographies of men and women whose lives illustrate one or more primary virtues or aspects of good character. The books are written for the young reader in middle school or junior high and include critical thinking questions, a summary chapter, and afterword to parents. The facts and events recorded in this book are true and based upon the most reliable research sources available. However, the authors have dramatized some scenes and dialogue to make the text more readable. In such cases, every effort was made to build the dialogue on a*

Table of Contents

Timeline

Biographical Milestone	Year	Historical Milestone

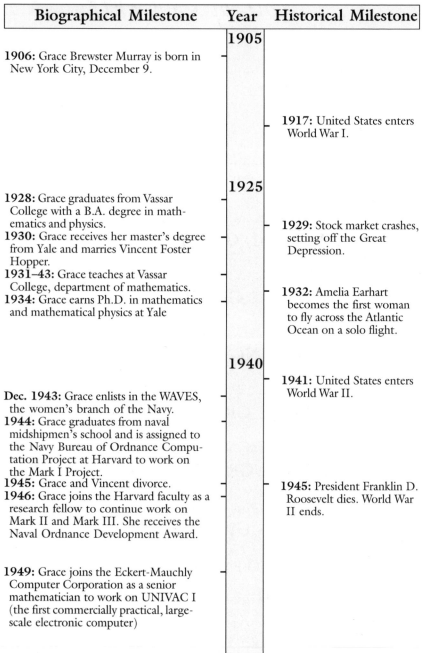

1906: Grace Brewster Murray is born in New York City, December 9.

1905

1917: United States enters World War I.

1925

1928: Grace graduates from Vassar College with a B.A. degree in mathematics and physics.
1930: Grace receives her master's degree from Yale and marries Vincent Foster Hopper.
1931–43: Grace teaches at Vassar College, department of mathematics.
1934: Grace earns Ph.D. in mathematics and mathematical physics at Yale

1929: Stock market crashes, setting off the Great Depression.

1932: Amelia Earhart becomes the first woman to fly across the Atlantic Ocean on a solo flight.

1940

1941: United States enters World War II.

Dec. 1943: Grace enlists in the WAVES, the women's branch of the Navy.
1944: Grace graduates from naval midshipmen's school and is assigned to the Navy Bureau of Ordnance Computation Project at Harvard to work on the Mark I Project.
1945: Grace and Vincent divorce.
1946: Grace joins the Harvard faculty as a research fellow to continue work on Mark II and Mark III. She receives the Naval Ordnance Development Award.

1945: President Franklin D. Roosevelt dies. World War II ends.

1949: Grace joins the Eckert-Mauchly Computer Corporation as a senior mathematician to work on UNIVAC I (the first commercially practical, large-scale electronic computer)

Historical Milestone	Year	Biographical Milestone
1950–53: Korean War.	1950	1952: Grace is promoted to rank of Commander, USN.
1960: John F. Kennedy is elected president.		1959: Grace begins teaching at the Moore School of Electrical Engineering at the University of Pennsylvania. COBOL, the first computer language for business, is launched.
Nov. 1963: President Kennedy is assassinated in Dallas, Texas.		1962: Grace is elected Fellow of the Institute of Electrical and Electronic Engineers.
1965: Black leader Malcolm X is assassinated.	1965	1964: Grace becomes staff scientist, Systems Programming, in the UNIVAC Division of Sperry-Rand Corporation.
		1966: Grace retires from the Navy reserve with the rank of commander. 1967: Navy recalls Grace to active duty.
1968: Martin Luther King, Jr. is assassinated.		1969: Data Processing Management Association elects Grace "Man of the Year." 1971: Grace retires from Sperry.
1974: President Richard Nixon resigns.		1973: Navy promotes Grace to rank of captain.
1980: Ronald Reagan is elected president.	1980	1983: Navy promotes Grace to rank of commodore.
		1985: Navy promotes Grace to rear admiral. 1986: Admiral Hopper retires from the Navy at age 79 and begins working for Digital Equipment Corporation.
1991: U.S.-led coalition defeats Iraq in the Persian Gulf War		1992: Grace Murray Hopper dies January 1 in her home in Arlington, Virginia, at the age of 86.

Prologue

❉

WORK

*W*het are you going to be when you grow up?"

When people ask that, they usually mean, "What work are you going to do?" That's an important question. You'll spend much of your lifetime working. Much of the difference you make in the world will come from your work. Working can make you miserable or delight you.

Who knows what work you will do? Of course, you want something interesting. Something that will help other people. Maybe you will do one job for a while and then find another that you like even better or that you can do right along with your first job. Maybe you will do something that nobody has even thought of yet. Maybe you will invent your own job.

That's the way it was with Grace Murray Hopper. She thought she might teach, and she did, and loved it. She certainly never imagined that she would grow up to be a computer pioneer; when she was born in 1906, computers didn't exist. She didn't dream that she would join the Navy, because that was only for men. In those days the Navy did not admit women, except nurses and (in World War I) a few clerks whom everyone called yeomanettes.

She did know that she liked numbers. So she set herself a goal of finding out all she could about them. The more she learned, the more interesting her work became.

Points to Ponder

♦ Some work is fun. Some is boring. How can you choose a job that you will really like?

♦ What is the difference between work and play? If you have a job that you like, is that work or play? When Rebecca Lobo earns money by shooting baskets, is she working or playing?

♦ Do the people around you enjoy their work? Do your teachers?

Chapter 1

CURIOUS GRACE

*I*n her family's summer cottage on Lake Wentworth in New Hampshire, back in 1913, six-year-old Grace Murray stood staring at her bedroom clock. "What makes it tick?" she wondered. "What makes the hands move? When I wind it up every night with the little lever on the back, what happens inside?" She tiptoed downstairs and got a screwdriver from her father's toolbox. Upstairs again, she unscrewed the back of the clock. Inside she found little

*Grace (on the left) at six years old, with her father, baby brother
Roger and sister Mary, at their summer cottage in Wolfeboro,
New Hampshire. (Courtesy: Dr. Roger Murray II, Wolfeboro,
New Hampshire)*

wheels and springs. Carefully she took these out, putting
the wheels in one pile and the springs in another. "I still
don't see what makes it work," she said to herself. "Maybe
if I put it back together again. . . ." But she couldn't.

"There's another clock in my little sister Mary's
bedroom. I'll try that one," she decided. The cottage
had seven bedrooms and seven clocks. Grace ended up
with seven little piles of wheels, seven little piles of springs
— and no whole clocks.

Of course, her parents were not happy about all those broken clocks. They sent Grace to her room to punish her, but they didn't forbid her to take clocks apart. "After this," they said, "you may work on clocks — but only one at a time."

"We have a bright, curious little girl," they told each other. "She loves gadgets and wants to find out how things work. She'll never be satisfied until she finds out."

They were right. All during her childhood, summers at her parents' Lake Wentworth cottage and winters in their New York City house, indoors and outdoors, playing or studying, Grace explored and tinkered, trying to find out how things worked.

Her parents encouraged her by giving her construction kits with little engines. With them she erected buildings and made elevators and wagons and no-name things that moved. She knitted and crocheted and sewed and hammered and sawed, making tiny chairs, tables, curtains and rugs for her dollhouse, and clothes for the dolls who lived in it. With puppets that she made, she acted out the Native American legends she read.

She loved to read, especially about girls who lived long ago. Louisa May Alcott's *Little Women* was a favorite. She reveled in adventure stories and dreamed about going adventuring herself. In Rudyard Kipling's *Just So Stories* she read about how things got started in the world — like how the alphabet was made. Every summer her school assigned her twenty books to read and write reports about.

All that reading made her want to learn more about history.

She begged her family for stories about her own ancestors, especially about those who had served their country in the military — like the one who had been a minuteman in the Revolutionary War. Most often, she asked for stories about her favorite great-grandfather, Alexander Wilson Russell. He had served in the U.S. Navy and risen to the rank of rear admiral. He was her hero.

Grace also explored the world of numbers, which she could see her family using every day. Walter Murray, her father, worked in insurance — an industry based on numbers. Her mother, Mary Murray, used arithmetic to pay bills and figure out how much the family had to spend and how much money they could save and invest. Her grandfather, a senior civil engineer for the city of New York, showed her how he used geometry. Sometimes he let her help measure distances: He sent her far down the street to hold a big, red-and-white-striped range pole (stadia rod) for the surveyors who worked for him.

"Hold it exactly straight," her grandfather told her. "If you don't, the surveyor will get the distances wrong."

At school Grace liked arithmetic, but she liked geometry even better. "When I did geometry problems," she said, "I could use all the colored pencils."

In those days long ago many people didn't think girls needed an education. Grace's parents didn't agree. They sent her and Mary to schools just as good as the one their younger brother, Roger, went to. They thought that both girls and boys ought to be educated in order to earn their own livings.

Grace's father said that he might or might not be able to leave his children money, but he could see that they were trained to take care of themselves. "Go to college," he said, "and then go to work so that you'll always know you can support yourself."

Grace's parents taught their daughters and son to depend on themselves in other ways, too. When Grace's sail canoe filled with water, her mother stood on shore and shouted, "Remember your great-grandfather, the admiral. Don't let your ship sink!" So Grace tipped the canoe over and, swimming hard, towed it to shore.

Her father, both of whose legs had to be amputated, always told his children, "If I can walk with two wooden legs and two canes, *you can do anything!*"

Points to Ponder

◆ What do you know about your own ancestors?

◆ What do you like to read about?

◆ Grace learned how to make useful things with her construction kits, and to how knit, crochet and sew. What skills would you like to learn?

Chapter 2

❖

PRACTICAL GRACE

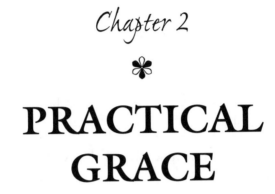

hen Grace graduated from high school in 1923, she chose to go to Vassar, at that time a college for women only. Then she hit a snag. She flunked the Latin part of her entrance exam for Vassar.

"Ouch," thought Grace. "How could this happen to me? I've always had top grades. *Now* what shall I do?"

"Never mind," said her folks. "You're a little young for college anyhow. We'll send you to prep school for a year, and then you can take the Vassar exams again."

She spent a year at the Hartridge School in New Jersey. For the first time, she lived away from home, plugging away at Latin and her other studies and learning to play hockey and basketball. At year's end she retook and passed the Latin exam, and in the fall of 1924, off she went to college.

At Vassar, because she still loved numbers, Grace decided to major in mathematics. "What are you going to do when you graduate?" everyone asked her. She didn't know.

"Maybe I'll teach math," she thought. "Or maybe I'll go to work for an insurance company, like my dad, figuring out probabilities: how long people are likely to live, how many trees a hurricane might blow down or how many oil spills a storm at sea might cause. I just don't know, but I bet I can do something interesting with numbers."

She loved her math courses but the more she studied, the more she wanted to explore other subjects. "I like to build things," she told her adviser. "I like gadgets and engines — useful things. I need to learn more about how things work. Does Vassar have any courses in engineering?"

"No," said her adviser. "Women don't usually study those things. We can't teach you to build bridges or put up buildings. We *can* teach you things that engineers need to know, though. We offer courses in physics, where you'll learn about light and energy and how they work. If you take electricity and electronics, you'll get to build complicated things like a spectroscope — a tool for measuring light waves."

Grace kept signing up for more and more courses. Remembering the way her parents used numbers, she took courses in business and economics. To satisfy her curiosity about the earth and plants, rocks and people, she sat in on courses in botany, geology and physiology.

For her, it wasn't enough to understand ideas or the theories she was studying. She also asked about how they applied in practice, in the world of work. "How can these theories help solve everyday problems?

I shall ever be grateful to Grace for tutoring me in physics when I failed the midterm. With her help, I suddenly began to understand the approach to science.

—A Vassar classmate, 1995

Soon Grace was helping other students who found their studies difficult — or didn't work as hard at them. In this way she discovered that she liked teaching.

"No wonder the students I tutor don't understand the theories we're studying," she said to herself. "They don't see how those ideas apply in real life. They don't see what use they are." So instead of just telling students how things work, explaining the theory, she showed them, in ways they couldn't forget. Once, to show her students how an object displaces water, she had them drop a classmate into a full bathtub. The water was displaced, all right, all over the floor!

In her college years, airplanes were still so new and so few that people got excited when they sighted one. She spent almost all her money to go up in a rickety, open-cockpit, single-engine airplane. The pilot eked out a living by barnstorming and touring the country giving ten-minute airplane rides, showing off his fancy stunt flying with tricks like looping the loop.

In 1928, Grace graduated from Vassar, receiving her bachelor of arts degree with honors. She was invited to join Phi Beta Kappa, a nationwide society for the best students. She also proved her father's theory that college would help her earn her own living. To her delight, her good record won her a scholarship so that she could keep on with her studies, this time at Yale University in New Haven, Connecticut.

After two years, she earned a master of arts degree at Yale. Now at last, after all that studying Grace was ready to begin her career. She was young to teach in college, only twenty-four. Vassar wanted her, though, this time not as a student but as an assistant — at a salary of $800 a year. As a member of the faculty, she remembered what she had learned when she was tutoring her classmates. Her students would learn more, she knew, if they saw a practical use for what they were studying. When she taught mathematics, she had her students plan a city and calculate how much it would cost to run, and how to raise the money. In her course on probabilities — what is mathematically most likely to happen — she had them predict which numbers would turn up when they threw a pair of dice.

In faculty meetings, Grace stood up for students who were having trouble. She once told a story about a faculty debate over whether freshmen who had four Ds at midyear should be made to leave college. A long, drawn-out argument over the proposal ended in a hurry when Grace stood up and announced that in her freshman year she herself had had four Ds at midyear.

Grace knew that she, herself, needed to study even more. To become a full professor, she must continue part time with her studies at Yale at the same time she taught at Vassar. Anyway, she *wanted* to learn more. "I will never stop learning," she said, "because I have an insatiable curiosity. People who don't keep on learning, die."

Points to Ponder

◆ When Grace was growing up, many people thought that girls should be taught to keep house instead of to work outside the home. How were you taught to think about that?

◆ What are you curious about? What do you want to learn?

◆ Who is your hero? Will knowing about her or him help you decide what work you want to do?

Chapter 3

PATRIOTIC GRACE

n 1928, the summer after she graduated from college, Grace Murray met Vincent Foster Hopper at Lake Wentworth. He was a young professor, just starting to teach English at New York University. They liked each other — a lot. Both of them enjoyed teaching and learning. Both were planning on further study. He teased her, though, claiming that even when they went out together, she thought more about math problems than she thought about him.

"You keep looking far away over my shoulder," he said, "and at the end of the evening you say, 'Aha, the answer is zero.' " All the same, they fell in love and married in 1930, soon after Grace got her master's degree.

They had happy times together. In many ways, they were lucky. They were married during the worst of the Great Depression, which began in 1929. At that time, one out of every four Americans could not find a job. Desperate people took any job, no matter how boring or how dangerous, no matter how long the hours, no matter how low the pay. Some college professors were digging ditches. Some families, some women and men on their own — even teenage boys and girls — traveled from place to place, looking for work. Many people did not have enough to eat, and many shivered in cold houses. Grandparents and parents, children and cousins often crammed together into one small house to save money on rent.

But Grace and Vincent were both employed. Grace's family gave them a beautiful wedding. They spent a long honeymoon traveling in Europe. When they came back, they built a house near Vassar. In the garage they kept a Model A Ford roadster — an open sports car with a cloth convertible top. Its one inside seat held two people, or three at a squeeze. Luggage went in the back compartment, though some roadsters had a rumble seat in the open air instead.

Despite all these luxuries, the Hoppers had problems that many other young couples didn't have. For most families in the 1930s, just one job mattered — the husband's. Other couples thought themselves lucky if either the husband or the wife had a job. But Grace and Vincent had two careers to think about, so they had little time to enjoy being with each other. It was difficult for them to be in the same place as much as they would have liked. He was teaching at New York University and studying for his doctorate at Columbia University in New York City; she was teaching at Vassar in Poughkeepsie and studying for her doctorate at Yale, in New Haven. They had what we would call today a "commuting marriage."

For about ten years they went along, both following their separate interests, both busy teaching and studying. While Grace plunged deeper and deeper into mathematics, Vincent read more and more of English literature. In 1934, when she was twenty-eight, she earned her last degree — a Ph.D. (doctor of philosophy) in mathematics. The young Hoppers didn't have any children. About 1940 they had to admit that things just weren't working out in their marriage. They agreed to live apart.

It was an unhappy time. As usual, working helped Grace Hopper and gave her something new to think about, for soon afterward her life changed dramatically, as she stepped into a whole new world of work.

"Rosie the Riveter," a popular song during World War II, inspired many women who supported American troops by going to work in munitions or aircraft plants. One such woman was Freda MacArthur, who worked as a router machine operator for the Boeing Aircraft Company. (Still Picture Branch: National Archives)

In December 1941, the Japanese, in a sneak attack, almost wiped out half the American Navy by bombing Pearl Harbor. Right away the United States declared war on Japan and its allies, Germany and Italy. American men rushed to recruiting offices to enlist in the Army, Navy, Coast Guard and Marines. American women filled the gaps the men left in offices and factories, making jeeps, ships and airplanes. People began singing about "Rosie the Riveter".

Grace's patriotism flamed. In World War I, she had been a teenager. About all she could do then to help was knit warm clothing for American soldiers and sailors. But now in World War II the United States needed women as well as men in its military services. Uncle Sam called on young women to sign up in the Navy as WAVES (Women Accepted for Volunteer Emergency Service). Thousands of women patriotically responded. Grace could have jumped up and cheered.

"Here's a chance to follow in the footsteps of my great-grandfather, the admiral," she thought. Never had she guessed that she would get to do that.

The Navy wasn't so sure. At thirty-six, Grace was too old, the Navy recruiters said. She was too skinny. At any rate, that's the way she told the story. Maybe they hesitated to accept her because they believed that during the war, math teachers, including Grace Hopper, should keep on teaching math. To win the war, the country needed thousands of mathematicians; Professor Hopper should help train them.

Grace, of course, didn't give up easily. She took a leave of absence from Vassar so that she could truthfully tell the Navy that she wasn't teaching math. She might be older than most Navy women and she might be skinny, but she could still do whatever the Navy needed done. She persisted, and finally the Navy decided that her skills and knowledge as a mathematician and a physicist were too valuable to reject.

The Navy signed her up as an officer candidate and sent her off to midshipmen's school at Smith College in Northampton, Massachusetts. There she and other women officers-to-be learned Navy terms, like "deck" for "floor," "cover" for "hat" and "hatch" instead of "door." They learned military courtesy, including how to salute. They studied Navy history and customs. They learned to identify different kinds of ships, submarines and airplanes. They wore smart, new uniforms, fashioned by a famous designer. Everywhere they went they marched: to meals, to classes, on errands, everywhere. It was a funny feeling for Grace to be a student again. After all, some of her classmates in the Navy were young women she had taught at Vassar.

She had always admired Navy people because of her great-grandfather. Now she found that she loved life in the Navy. She enjoyed wearing the uniform.

"How could I not join the Navy," she asked, "when I love the color blue?" She was proud to have the world know that she was a Navy woman.

In the Navy, she learned a lesson that she never forgot. Loyalty was a two-way street — loyalty up and loyalty down. As an officer low in the chain of command, a mere lieutenant, she would be led by lieutenant commanders, commanders, captains, commodores and admirals. All were officers higher up than she was. She herself would lead a crew of sailors and ensigns who reported to her. She owed respect and obedience to the

Grace as a commander in the U.S. Navy in 1957. (Courtesy: Dr. Roger Murray II, Wolfeboro, NH)

officers above her, and she took responsibility for her crew.

Her pride swelled when she graduated and was commissioned. The first thing the new Lieutenant Hopper did was to buy a big bouquet of flowers for her great-grandfather, Admiral Russell. She laid them on his grave. In the 1940s, she reassured him, it was all right for a woman to join the Navy.

"Otherwise, if I hadn't told him," she joked, "he would have rolled over in his grave."

Grace had found a home in the Navy. She loved and respected it all her life. She might have earned more money in other jobs. That didn't matter. Whenever during her long life she was honored, she always said, "I've already received the highest award I'll ever receive, no matter how long I live, no matter how many more jobs I may have. That has been the privilege and the responsibility of serving very proudly in the United States Navy."

Points to Ponder

◆ What did Grace Hopper like most about her work? Earning money? Solving difficult problems? Being with interesting people?

◆ How much do you know about World War II? Did any of your relatives serve in the military?

◆ Do you think Grace should have gone into the military? Or should she have kept on teaching at Vassar, the way the Navy at first wanted her to?

Chapter 4

PIONEERING GRACE

All her life, Grace Hopper was a pioneer. When many little girls only played house, she built toy houses. When most young women did not go to college, her parents sent her. When few women went to graduate school, she earned her Ph.D. — and in mathematics, a subject that few women then studied.

Of course, Grace was curious about where the Navy would send her and what they would tell her to do. She eagerly ripped open her first orders: "Report to Commander Howard Aiken, Navy Bureau of Ordnance Computation Project, Harvard University, Cambridge, Massachusetts." "For goodness' sake," she asked herself, "what is this computation project? What does the Navy think I can do there?"

Grace didn't know it, but the Navy was giving her another chance to pioneer — by putting her into computing, where everyone was a pioneer. Women and men alike, everyone who worked with computers was exploring. They were wondering how much they could make computers do. How many tasks could they make easier? How could people talk to computers? How could computers talk to people? Would computers ever be able to think like people? How fast could computers work? We still don't know the answers to some of these questions.

Although by the 1940s women were doing almost every kind of work, people still thought of some jobs as women's and others as men's. For instance, they thought of doctors as men and nurses as women. Computing, however, was wide open for people with trained minds, people who understood math and science. People like that were so hard to find that employers didn't worry so much about their gender. Dr. Hopper had proved she could do the mathematical work. Her degrees and the

The English mathematician, Charles Babbage, conceived the first digital computer in 1834.

papers she had written were proof. But at this point, she knew almost nothing about computers.

Grace didn't even know that most people give the credit for designing the first digital computer to Charles Babbage, an English mathematician, engineer and inventor. When, in 1834, he thought up his "analytical engine," the machines of the time weren't good enough to build it. Without electricity, his computer would have needed six steam engines to run it. Besides, nobody wanted it — even scientists and engineers said, "Who needs it? The slide rule [invented in 1654] is good enough."

[When Grace Hopper arrived at Harvard she] didn't know the difference between a relay and a tomato basket. But she was a fast learner.

—Ensign Richard M. Bloch,
a co-worker at Harvard, 1997

Luckily, among Babbage's friends was Augusta Ada King, Countess of Lovelace (1815–52) and daughter of Lord Byron. Even though his computer was never built, she understood its capabilities and how it could be used. In 1843, she worked through the thirty notebooks that Babbage had filled with plans for his invention and wrote a series of notes that explained his analytical engine.

Exactly 100 years later, in 1943, Howard Aiken was working on the first large-scale, digital computer, the Mark I. He was in a hurry, partly because he wanted to see what it could do and partly because it might help the United States and its allies win World War II. Aiken thought of Charles Babbage as one of his intellectual ancestors. Before he built his Mark I, he studied Babbage's plans for the analytical engine. The Mark I, run by electricity, was fifty-one feet long, nearly as long as a basketball court, eight feet high and eight feet wide. It weighed five tons: 10,000 pounds. It seemed wonderful to everybody then that the Mark I could do three additions per second. That's faster than most people can add, but it is ridiculously slow compared to what any laptop computer can do at the end of the twentieth century.

When Grace walked into the laboratory that housed the Mark I, Aiken said, "Where the hell have you been for the last two months?" Of course she had been where the Navy ordered, at midshipmen's school.

"I told them you didn't need that," said Aiken. "We've got to get to work." He introduced her to the Mark I, saying, "That's a computing engine."

Grace stared at it. "That's an impressive beast," she gasped. She fell in love with it at first sight, itching to take it apart. Later she said, "I always loved a good gadget. When I met Mark I, it was the biggest, fanciest gadget I'd ever seen. I had to find out how it worked."

Grace didn't take apart the Mark I, but she did find out how it worked and she learned to program it. With her team, she taught the Mark I to work out tables to help naval gunners aim just right. The big "computing engine" did millions of calculations for mines, self-propelled rockets and the atomic bomb.

She faced a problem with her crew of young, male ensigns, however. Even in the Navy, crews sometimes give officers a hard time if they don't respect them. Before she came, someone had told them that a white-haired, old-lady schoolteacher would be joining them. They

The immense Harvard Mark I computer was considered a "fast" analytical engine during the 1940s. (Courtesy: Dr. Roger Murray II, Wolfeboro, NH)

didn't like the idea of working for a woman. They bribed each other to keep from having to sit next to her. Grace soon showed them that she knew what she was doing and that she could learn more. She proved that she could lead them and make their work more interesting. She tackled jobs that other people didn't want to do.

Besides, she made the ensigns laugh — especially when a group of admirals came to visit the Mark I on a day when it was shutting down every few seconds and they hadn't yet found the trouble. The whole time the admirals were there, Grace leaned against the big machine and kept her finger on the start button to keep it running.

The admirals didn't notice that the Mark I was making one mistake after another, and they left thinking they had seen a run without an error.

After that, her crew worked long and hard. Just keeping the Mark I — and later the Mark II and the Mark III — running could be a problem. For all their size, early computers were delicate. A sharp change in temperature or a speck of dust in the wrong place could throw them off. Even at night the scientists had to baby-sit their big machines. Sometimes they would sleep on their desks all night. "Chaperoning these two damned computers," Grace called it.

Once, troubleshooting the Mark II, she used the mirror from her purse to find a moth inside the computer. They fished it out with tweezers — the first "debugging" in the history of computing.

We respected [Grace Hopper's] brilliant mind and were impressed with her Navy career as developer of their new computer system. We also liked her — she had a generous nature and common sense, but refrained from giving advice.

—A Vassar student, 1997

Grace with Commander Howard Aiken in 1943. (Courtesy: Dr. Roger Murray II, Wolfeboro, NH)

Navy orders kept them all hopping. Sometimes those orders seemed impossible. Grace often reminded her crew of the motto of the Navy's Seabees, who built airstrips and roads for the Navy: "The difficult we do right away. The impossible takes a little longer." All the same, when Aiken told Grace to write a computer manual herself, she gasped, "I can't."

But, Commander Aiken reminded Grace, "you're in the Navy now. In the Navy, the only acceptable answer to an order is 'Yes, sir' or 'Yes, ma'am.' " She wrote the book.

In 1945, as World War II neared its end, Grace was going through a bleak, dismal time, probably the worst time in her private life. Her marriage to Vincent was ending in divorce. Maybe Vincent and Grace had just grown apart as they followed their different interests. Grace didn't like to talk about the breakup, so nobody knows for sure. In any case, though, Grace did not seek the divorce; she did not want it. She was heartbroken. For a while she almost despaired, looking for ways to regain her belief in herself as an attractive person.

Points to Ponder

◆ How was Grace Hopper like Charles Babbage? How was she like Augusta Ada King, Countess of Lovelace?

◆ What do you do when people tell you that something is "impossible"? When people say something is "impossible," does it usually mean it just hasn't been figured out yet?

Chapter 5

✳

CREATIVE GRACE

orse was still to come. In 1946, with World War II over, her beloved Navy told Grace they didn't need her any more for full-time work. She was, they said, too old. She was facing the failure of her marriage and the blasting of her ambitions for a Navy career. Inside herself, she must have known that work was the best thing for her, work that would take her mind off her troubles.

The Navy's decision was an obstacle she couldn't budge. She had to find a way around it. She couldn't stay on active duty, but she stayed in the Naval Reserve — the part of the Navy the nation calls on when it's needed. This decision obligated her to set aside some of her time to do whatever the Navy ordered. That way she could take courses to learn things that would be useful to the Navy and if they needed her again, she'd be ready.

Although she still felt sad and hurt, she grinned and said, "It's better to be told you're too old when you're forty because then you go through the experience and it doesn't bother you again."

The Naval Reserve wasn't a full-time job, however. Grace thought about going back to Vassar to teach. Instead, she decided to go on as a civilian helping Aiken build the Mark III, which was to be fifty times faster than the Mark I. Computers, she thought, were even more fun than teaching.

It's hard to believe now, but in the late 1940s hardly anyone thought that the world would need many more than 100 or so computers, if that many. In 1943, the chairman of IBM (International Business Machines) said, "I think there is a world market for maybe five computers." The scientists and mathematicians building them thought of computers mainly as something to help them solve problems in their own work. Few ever wondered how offices and factories might use computers.

Back then, who could imagine ordinary people using computers to do income taxes, buy airplane tickets or learn Spanish? As for playing games on the computer — anyone who even dreamed of it would know that was absurd. Of course, there were no modems, or e-mail, no Internet and no World Wide Web. Not even CD-ROMS.

Then, too, only mathematicians and other scientists understood enough about computers to know what they could do, or picture what they might do in the future. No one else knew how to talk to or program them. Businesspeople and other nonscientists could not even imagine what computers might do for them.

[Grace Hopper's] real strength [was in speaking to management] in terms they could understand.

—Betty Holberton, computer expert, 1997

In short, businesspeople knew what they needed done, but they didn't know that computers could do it; mathematicians and scientists knew what the computers of the day could do, but they didn't know what businesspeople needed.

Aiken, however, was already thinking about what the computer could do for businesspeople. He ordered Grace to write a program for Prudential Insurance Company. That assignment set her to wondering: Who else could use computers? What programs would store managers, factory workers and travel agents need? Most important of all, could computers learn to understand and respond in English?

"Impossible," said most people at the laboratory. "It just can't be done." Her bosses agreed. They did not want her to spend her time trying to make the computer understand everyday English. It irked them when she kept talking about it.

Grace wouldn't give up, so, in 1949, she decided to take another job. Eckert-Mauchly Corporation in Philadelphia offered her a position as senior mathematician to work on their Universal Automatic Computer (UNIVAC). This was the first commercial, large-scale electronic computer. Only fourteen feet long, less than a third of the size of the Mark I, it worked 1,000 times faster.

Most of her friends thought Grace was making a mistake when she agreed to join Eckert-Mauchly. The company was not yet firmly on its feet. Maybe it would go broke. Grace knew just how great the risk was, and she thought about what she would do if things didn't work out. Then she said, "It's much more fun to stick your neck out and take chances. Dare and do!"

The company certainly didn't look like much. It was in an old knitting mill, between a cemetery and a junkyard. "We used to say," Grace joked, "that if UNIVAC didn't work, we were going to throw it out one side into the junkyard, and we were going to jump out the other side into the cemetery."

In other ways, though, Eckert-Mauchly was a wonderful place to work because its employees had a lot of say in deciding what they would work on and how they would go about it. Even the youngest employee felt that all the people in the company were learning and trying out new things together. They were a team. With no existing tools to debug programs, programmers worked closely with engineers, building and improving UNIVAC as they went along.

"Even though I was just a beginner," Adele Mildred Koss remembered, "I was allowed to figure out what I wanted to do, try it out, consult with anyone I liked. That's the kind of independence that Grace gave us; you were allowed to do whatever you felt you had to and nobody said, 'Well this is the way you should do it — this is the logic you should use.' It was just, 'Let's see what you can come up with.' "

Grace kept asking, "Can you find a way to make the computer do what you're doing now by hand?" And, "Now we know we have this powerful thing here, what new problem could be solved with this?" She didn't manage or manipulate people. She led them. She got them so excited about what they could do that they worked hard — sometimes all day and all night long.

Grace had to go out looking for programmers. There just weren't enough of them around. So she hired women and men who liked to work crossword puzzles and read mystery stories — problem solvers. Then she taught them to program computers.

She liked to hire young people, because they didn't often say, "That's the way we've always done it," or "It can't be done." They didn't know that something had always been thought impossible. They just went ahead and did it.

Grace always felt that if you wanted some results or new approaches, give the problem to someone who is young and does not have a preconceived notion of the way they can do it.

—Adele Mildred Koss, computer expert, 1993

She looked especially for women programmers. Most people find it more exciting to crack a puzzle than to put the last pieces in. They want to get on to a new puzzle. "But," said Hopper, "women don't just cook the meat and potatoes and leave it at that. They learn to finish up the meal and get it on the plates, ready to eat." She trusted them to get computer programs ready to use.

In 1952, Eckert-Mauchly — which had become part of the Sperry Corporation — promoted Grace to systems engineer and director of automatic programming. Despite her success, life at this time had its problems. For every program they made, programmers were spending long hours copying out certain commands in code. Worse still, all that copying led to lots of errors, because, she said, "programmers are lousy adders." When Grace talked about getting the computer to do that job, she heard the same old cry, "That's impossible."

"Well, let's take it step-by-step," she said. First she encouraged programmers to put all those coded commands into a library that they could share. Then she created a program that translated math codes into machine language, so that programmers could store codes on magnetic tape and recall them when they were needed. Grace had made the first compiler.

She honestly believed that the capability of the computer was endless and transformed any problem solving.

—Adele Mildred Koss, computer expert, 1993

The years Grace spent with UNIVAC — expanding the computer's potential and experimenting with teaching it English — prepared the way for the first English-like computer language designed for business. In 1957, Grace and her staff developed a more complex compiler, FLOW-MATIC, a business program written in English and then transposed into binary code (a series of zeros and ones)

In 1966, after twenty-three years of service, the Navy asked Grace to retire. Grace was saddened by this request, as the Navy had been such a big part of her life for so many years. (Courtesy: Dr. Roger Murray II, Wolfeboro, NH)

that helped UNIVAC understand twenty English statements. As she proved, UNIVAC could just as easily learn to understand French or German. This was the first computer language employing words. The manual for running FLOW-MATIC had the first complete set of commands, including *add, execute* and *stop*. In 1959, FLOW-MATIC led to the more complex COBOL (Common Business-Oriented Language), which also was based on a series of commands instead of mathematical codes. Many people call Grace the "grandmother of COBOL."

NOBODY'S PERFECT

Grace Hopper was a strong, self-confident woman. Quite correctly, she believed that she could do whatever she needed to. But she failed in one thing. She never did stop smoking. It's not surprising that she started to smoke. When she was young, most people did, for few understood the dangers of smoking. The sad thing is that Grace never managed to stop. She always told young people, "Don't start."

In that same year, Grace also began teaching at the University of Pennsylvania. By now she had gained a lot of self-confidence and derring-do. When her boss refused her request for something she thought she needed to do her job, she took another risk. "OK," she said, "I'll quit. I'll clean out my desk and leave this afternoon." He laughed and reminded her that she had already used the same threat once that year. She said later, "I always figured I could get a job as a waitress. It would have been temporary. You must stand on your own two feet. That's half the fun."

In 1964, Sperry-Rand again promoted Grace, this time to staff scientist, systems programming. Until late 1966, Grace enjoyed her complicated life: working for Sperry-Rand and teaching at the University of Pennsylvania. Working with younger people and teaching them always delighted her. She talked about helping them, listening to them, learning from them.

"Anyone half my age," she said, "is young."

All these years, along with her work for Sperry-Rand and her teaching, Grace was also keeping up with her duties in the Naval Reserve. It was unusual for anyone to stay in the Reserve so long. Most military people retire when they are forty-five or fifty. She was sixty. The Navy rules say that people can retire with a pension after twenty years, and she had been in the service for twenty-three years. No longer a lieutenant, she now held the rank of commander. But in 1966, the Navy told her to retire. So twenty years after the Navy had first told her that she was too old, she retired on December 31, 1966. "That was the saddest day of my life," she said.

Points to Ponder

◆ What do you think computers will be able to do in ten years that they cannot do now? What would you like them to do?

◆ Grace led the members of her work teams by asking questions rather than handing out orders. How do you help other people on your teams?

Chapter 6

❀

AMAZING GRACE

G uess what? The Navy soon found it couldn't do without Grace Hopper! COBOL still wasn't perfect and Navy people were having trouble using it; the Navy's payroll program hadbeen rewritten 823 times! They needed a real expert, so they asked Grace to come back and help them for six months. Happily, on August 1, 1967, she returned to full-time, active duty. In her own words, "I came running — I always do when the Navy sends for me."

At the Pentagon in Washington, D.C., the Navy ordered Grace to perfect COBOL, and then get everyone in the Navy to use it. She knew how allergic people are to change.

"The first job — perfecting COBOL — is finite; I can finish it up," she said. "The second job — getting everyone to use it — is infinite, endless. But I will be glad to try."

Grace Hopper was a feisty old salt who gave off an aura of power.

—From a report on Grace's appearance at the
1987 Navy Micro Conference

At age sixty, after so many years of teaching and computer experience, Grace felt sure of herself and ready to tell people what she thought. She was good at her work, and she knew it. She was a peppery, spirited maverick.

"I'm a boat-rocker," Grace said. To shake up people's minds and keep them from doing things the same way all the time, she brought into her Pentagon office a clock that ran backwards. The

Grace was happy to return to active duty with the Navy in 1967. As head of the Navy programming section of the office of the Chief of Naval Operations, she discusses a project with a fellow employee. (Courtesy: Dr. Roger Murray II, Wolfeboro, NH)

hands went in the opposite direction from those of other clocks. Her backwards clock told the right time. People just had to learn to read it "wrong" way around.

Sometimes when Navy rules got in her way, it was too bad for Navy rules. Commander Hopper hadn't acted like that when she was a lowly lieutenant. Now she had clout, clout that came from her rank and from all that she knew and all that she had done.

Grace Murray Hopper has challenged at every turn the dictates of mindless bureaucracy.

—John F. Lehman Jr.,
Secretary of the Navy, 1986

Grace liked to do things simply and directly. She moved papers from office to office in a child's little red wagon, instead of in Navy carts. When she first walked into her empty Navy office in the Pentagon, she was handed lots of forms to fill out to get her furniture. Instead, she told her crew to scrounge for it in other offices.

"Liberate what we need. Set it free. It's easier to apologize after you do something than to ask permission to do it," she said.

"I don't want young people to wait around for permission," Grace said. "I want them to go ahead and do things. If it is to do something which is constructive and which will contribute, do it."

She told a story about a young lieutenant junior grade who was ordered to a small ship: "The Navy thought it was too small to have a computer. He took his own computer aboard with him. In a very short time, he had the ship's records in his computer. He was getting all the reports out on time; everything was running beautifully. When he was transferred, the captain had to buy his computer, as the ship could not run without it any more. Way to go!"

Grace's style annoyed some people — especially, she thought, because she always insisted on understanding things. When the engineers began talking about "nanoseconds," she said, "I don't know what you mean." She didn't think a lot of other people did either. "Show me," she said. She knew that a nanosecond is a billionth of a second, but what is a billionth? Who could imagine it? The engineers cut off a piece of wire 11.8 inches long, the distance electricity can travel in a billionth of a second. Grace had her nanosecond.

Later, she got lots of nanoseconds and passed them out when she spoke, so that everyone in the audience could understand. One came in handy when she had to tell an admiral why it took so long to get a message to a satellite.

"I had to explain to him," she said, "that there are many, many nanoseconds between earth and the satellite."

When the engineers began talking about a picosecond, a trillionth of a second, she told people, "Go to a fast-food restaurant and you'll get a packet of picoseconds there. They're labeled 'pepper.'" She meant that the distance that electricity can travel in a trillionth of a second is so small that it would look like a single grain of pepper.

Her vision has been a "fire" in the imagination of many who made things happen in computers. She was indeed a wonderful, brilliant example for me.

—Commander Ginny Mullen,
USN (Ret.), 1997

Grace's six-month tour of active duty in the Navy kept getting stretched further and further. Her duties multiplied. In the universities, in the business world, in the military, thousands of people recognized her in the crisp Navy uniform she loved to wear. She joked a lot and made a good story of whatever she did. People picked up and passed on these stories, laughing and marveling about the little old lady who was teaching the Navy how to use comruters better; the little old lady who told the Navy's top people just what she thought; the little old lady the Navy couldn't get along without.

Grace with students and faculty of Brewster Academy in Wolfeboro, New Hampshire, after the dedication ceremony of the Grace Murray Hopper Center for Computer Learning in November 1983. (Courtesy: Brewster Academy, Wolfeboro, NH)

About 200 days a year, Grace lectured to computer specialists at military bases. As her fame spread, other departments of the U.S. government, businesses and schools asked her to speak to their people. Those lectures kept her busy another 100 days or so. That's hard work. Over the years, she earned $34,000 in outside lecture fees, but she didn't keep a cent of it. She gave it to Navy Relief, to help sailors and their families when they needed it.

One stop on Grace's lecture tour was Brewster Academy, a private school in Wolfeboro, New Hampshire, the town where Grace's family had a summer home during her youth. The students and faculty were so inspired by Grace's knowledge that a computer center was eventually established at the academy. In 1983, the Grace Murray Hopper Center for Computer Learning was opened.

With all this speaking and consulting, she had to travel tens of thousands of miles a year. Some people who saw her in airports just couldn't believe that this old woman in uniform was a naval officer. Some thought she was a security guard. And when she told an immigration officer that she was in the Navy, he said, "You must be the oldest one they've got."

He was right. Before she retired, she became the oldest person on active duty in the Navy. In 1985, the Navy promoted her to rear admiral — just like her great-grandfather-hero, Admiral Russell.

[Hopper] is in the chain of command that runs from the commander in chief to the secretary of defense to the secretary of the navy, across to the lone woman.

—Morley Safer on Sixty Minutes, 1983

Finally, in 1986, when she was seventy-nine years old, Admiral Hopper retired from the Navy. By then she

Grace with President Ronal Reagan at a state dinner at the White House in 1986. (Courtesy: Dr. Roger Murray II, Wolfeboro, NH)

had received far more honors than she could remember, both in the United States and abroad. She wound up with forty-seven honorary degrees. In a White House ceremony, President Ronald Reagan gave her the National Medal of Technology for her contributions in developing "the machine that assisted the power of the brain rather than muscle." But no honor pleased her as much as the

Naval Ordnance Development Award, given her back in 1946. She thought it meant, "You're on the right track. Keep up the good work."

On her retirement, the Navy celebrated her forty-three years of service with a special ceremony on the USS *Constitution* — "Old Ironsides," its crew dressed in 1812 uniforms. The oldest ship in the Navy was all decked out to honor the oldest sailor in the Navy.

"Do you realize," she asked a sailor there, "I'm the last of the World War II WAVES to leave active duty?"

NOBODY'S PERFECT

Grace Hopper may have collected more than her share of honors. Without meaning to, she may not always have admitted how much that she achieved came from teamwork. Adele Mildred Koss said, "There is some concern that Grace got more credit than she should have. In many cases a lot of people contributed to these ideas. I don't think it was her doing. It was just that she was such a strong personality that I think she might have become the focal point for this kind of recognition, no matter what."

On deck of the USS *Constitution,* Grace is given a bouquet of flowers at a special ceremony held in honor of her retirement from the Navy in 1985. (Courtesy: Dr. Roger Murray II, Wolfeboro, NH)

Even though she was seventy-nine years old — fourteen years beyond the normal retirement age in the business world — her experience and expertise promptly landed her a job offer from another computer corporation. This time she went to work as a special consultant for the Digital Equipment Corporation. "I'll try to push them into the future," she said when she accepted the position.

Grace died in 1992, when she was eighty-six. As she had asked, the Navy gave her a funeral with full military honors: a horse-drawn, flag-draped caisson, ruffles and flourishes, a rifle volley and the playing of taps.

"It would please my Scottish ancestors," she explained, "to have the Navy pay for my funeral."

"A ship in port is safe," Grace Hopper often said. "But that's not what ships are for. Be good ships. Sail out to sea, and do new things." Her ship never stayed in port for long.

Now, sailors on a 500-foot Navy destroyer call their ship "Amazing Grace." Commissioned in 1997, the USS *Hopper* is armed with far more computers than guns. Its coat of arms displays a single white star to represent her rank of rear admiral, a golden lion for her Scottish heritage and the ship's motto, *Aude et effice* — "Dare and do."

[Grace Hopper] has done more than any other person in computer technology to bring together people to share their knowledge. Largely because of her efforts, programming moved ahead quickly to the point where people who were not computer experts could use and program society's newest tool.

—Laura Greene,
author of *Computer Pioneers*, 1985

Points to Ponder

◆ Grace, like her Harvard boss, Howard Aiken, knew how hard it is to get people to think in new ways. Aiken always said not to worry about people stealing your ideas. "If it's original," he said, "you will have to ram it down their throats." Why do you think people find it difficult to accept new ideas?

◆ Was Grace lucky? How much did preparing herself and working hard have to do with her luck?

◆ Grace called herself a "boat-rocker." Is rocking the boat something to brag about?

Epilogue

✤

SUMMING UP
A LIFE

eople divide their time and energy
between their private lives and
their work. Even though Grace
Hopper's marriage didn't work out, she enjoyed her
private life. She stayed close to her sister and brother,
and to their children and grandchildren. She knitted for
her nieces and nephews and their children while she read

and watched TV — all at the same time. Of course she stored her knitting instructions on a computer. On her own time, she studied early American history.

But more than most people, Grace lived in her work. She thought it was exciting, and worth doing. She knew that what she did mattered. She took pride in the thousands of young people she had taught. She loved the challenges her work offered. She loved the opportunities to do something new and different.

Grace Hopper has been one of the most engaging and colorful personalities of computer history, a spokesperson, an educator, a strong-willed dynamo who has loved two things above all else, computers and the U.S. Navy.

—Robert Slater, *Portraits in Silicon,* 1987

We remember Grace Hopper for being the grandmother of COBOL and for helping to make the computer useful to many people. When so many other experts were thinking only about how computers could help the few, she was figuring out how they could help the many. Her insistence that computers could solve almost any problem led to user-friendly computers.

Commissioned on September 6, 1997, the USS Hopper *is often called "Amazing Grace" by the sailors who serve on her in honor of Grace Murray Hopper. (Courtesy: Roger Murray II, Wolfeboro, New Hampshire)*

In 1977, Ken Olsen, the president, chairman and founder of Digital Equipment Corporation, said, "There is no reason anyone would want a computer in their home." Grace knew better. She argued that just as Henry Ford's Model T had transformed the way people lived at the beginning of the twentieth century, so micro-computers were transforming the way people lived at its end.

"I remind people of what happened when we got the Model T Fords," Grace said. "Up until that time, we had the dirt roads. Then came the

Model Ts. They cost between $300 and $600, and people started to own cars — and the whole world changed. We now have the Model Ts of the computer industry. The microcomputers have made it possible for people to go out and buy a computer and have it in their home. And we are going to see a revolution, starting with the microcomputers, just as great as was created by the Model T Ford. We are now at the very beginning of what will be the largest industry in the United States."

She saw only one limit for computers. "No computer," she said, "will ever ask a reasonable new question. People have to think up the new questions."

Grace took every opportunity to challenge people young and old to consider the infinite possibilities of technology.

—Kenneth H. Olsen,
president of Digital Equipment, 1983

AFTERWORD

TO PARENTS

This book teaches your child about the remarkable Grace Murray Hopper and the virtues she personifies — especially the joys of working and studying, the importance of serving one's country and the courage to do something different. Along the way it also shows your daughter or son — most of whose life will be spent in the twenty-first century — what it was like to live in the twentieth.

You can help your child learn these lessons by talking with her or him about the meaning of Grace's life and work. You can add to it from your own life and experience. What have you found rewarding in your work? What do you find gives you a sense of accomplishment?

"Points to Ponder" at the end of each chapter are good jumping-off places for discussion. You can talk with your youngster about how important Grace's virtues and strong points have been for you and for people you have known. But don't neglect the sidebars entitled "Nobody's Perfect." Young people need to know that everyone makes mistakes and has faults.

Young people love to hear stories about what life was like when their parents were young. Remember that your child has never lived in a world without computers; you can describe that world. What about typewriters, carbon paper, onionskin, white-out and telegrams? What about the games you used to play and the toys you played with?

Finally, you can use the references to earlier times to interest your child in history; help him or her to imagine what living seventy-five years ago was like. For instance, you could use the description of the car the Hoppers owned as young married people to discuss when cars and airplanes came into general use. Let your children know how much the world has changed in your lifetime, and you'll be preparing them (and yourself) for the even faster pace of change they will see in theirs.

BIBLIOGRAPHY

Billings, Charlene W. *Grace Hopper: Navy Admiral and Computer Pioneer.* Hillside, NJ: Enslow Publishers, 1989.

Greene, Laura. *Computer Pioneers.* New York: Franklin Watts, 1985.

Slater, Robert. *Portraits in Silicon.* Cambridge, MA: MIT Press, 1987.

Whitelaw, Nancy. *Grace Hopper: Programming Pioneer.* New York: W. H. Freeman, 1995.

Toole, Betty A. *Ada, the Enchantress of Numbers: A Selection from the Letters of Lord Byron's Daughter and Her Description of the First Computer.* Mill Valley, CA: Strawberry Press, 1992.

GLOSSARY

binary code. A series of zeros and ones placed in a certain order that computers can understand.

bureaucracy. Government administration by officials following a fixed set of procedures. Such officials are often believed to be unimaginative and inflexible.

chaperone. A person, especially an older or married woman, who accompanies young, unmarried people to supervise their behavior.

derring-do. Daring action or reckless courage.

dynamo. A forceful, energetic person.

finite. Limited, capable of being completed.

infinite. Endless, unlimited.

insatiable. Constantly wanting more.

maverick. A person who takes an independent stand.

midshipman. A student in training to be a naval officer.

Ph.D. Doctor of Philosophy, the highest degree that universities award.

physics. The science dealing with the properties, changes, interactions, etc. of matter and energy, like electricity, heat, optics, mechanics and the atomic scale of nature.

ponder. Think over.

preconceive. Form an opinion in advance.

probabilities. A form of mathematics that figures out the number of times something will probably occur.

relay. An electromagnetic device set off by changes in one electric current and controlling a larger current, or setting off other devices in the same or another electric current.

slide rule. A ruler with a sliding piece, both parts marked with number scales, used to calculate mathematical equations.

spectra. A series of colored bands arranged in the order of their wavelengths.

spectroscope. An optical instrument used for forming spectra.